Success With
Challenging Students

Practical Skills for Counselors
Jeffrey A. Kottler, Series Editor

Brief Counseling That Works: A Solution-Focused Approach for School Counselors
Gerald B. Sklare

Deciphering the Diagnostic Codes: A Guide for School Counselors
W. Paul Jones

Success With Challenging Students
Jeffrey A. Kottler

Jeffrey A. Kottler

Success With
Challenging Students

CORWIN PRESS, INC.
A Sage Publications Company
Thousand Oaks, California

Originally published as *Succeeding With Difficult Students.*

For information address:

 Corwin Press, Inc.
A Sage Publications Company
2455 Teller Road
Thousand Oaks, California 91320
e-mail: order@corwin.sagepub.com

SAGE Publications Ltd.
6 Bonhill Street
London EC2A 4PU
United Kingdom

SAGE Publications India Pvt. Ltd.
M-32 Market
Greater Kailash I
New Delhi 110 048 India

Printed in the United States of America

Library of Congress Cataloging-in-Publication Data

Kottler, Jeffrey A.
    Success with challenging students / Jeffrey A. Kottler.
        p.   cm. — (Practical skills for counselors)
    Includes bibliographical references and index.
        ISBN 0-8039-6652-0 (pbk. : acid-free paper). — ISBN 0-8039-6651-2
(cloth : acid-free paper)
        1. Educational counseling—United States.   2. Problem children—
Counseling of—United States.   3. Problem children—Education—
United States.   I. Title.   II. Series.
LB1027.5.K665   1996
371.4′6—dc21   96-51272

This book is printed on acid-free paper.

97 98 99 00 01 10 9 8 7 6 5 4 3 2 1

Corwin Press Production Editor: S. Marlene Head
Editorial Assistant: Nicole Fountain
Typesetter: Rebecca Evans
Cover Designer: Marcia R. Finlayson
Indexer: Mary Kidd

Contents

Preface

This book, designed for school counselors and teachers who use
counseling skills in their daily interactions, is about those students who are perceived as the most challenging with whom to work.
It provides counselors with a model for understanding why some
students appear to be so resistant, unmotivated, and difficult, as well
as a number of practical strategies for changing established dysfunctional patterns.

Unique Features

In traditional educational training, school personnel have not been
prepared to deal with the challenging problems that they must too
often face today: gangs, violence, sexual abuse, addictions, and ob-
structiveness on a level that has never been seen before. Whereas
research and theoretical models are invaluable in helping guide our
behavior, what counselors and teachers have been crying for the
most are techniques and practices they can actually apply to make a
significant difference.

This book brings together most of what is known about the subject of difficult students—specifically, students who are needy, hostile, unmotivated, bored, withdrawn, isolated, inarticulate, manipulative, or attention seeking. Based on the literature, as well as extensive interviews with counselors in the field, this book offers a number of things that school personnel can do differently in the ways they approach these students, mobilize resources, and metabolize the inevitable stress that comes from these interactions.

Contents of the Book

In the first chapter, we look at those students who counselors see as being their most difficult. Although there is some consensus on this subject—for instance, children who are hostile, manipulative, withdrawn, or unmotivated—there are also wide differences in how challenging cases are defined. We come to recognize early on that counselors' ways of identifying students as difficult depend as much on their own perceptions and personal issues as on the child's behavior.

Chapter 2 looks at the question of why some children act so belligerently, obstructively, and uncooperatively. Until you can figure out what students are getting out of their behavior—the significance of their actions within their particular cultural, peer, and familial contexts—it is not possible to develop effective interventions.

The third chapter helps you to look inward before you explore creative things you can do to break through impasses with difficult students. Why do certain children get underneath your skin? What in you is getting in the way of being more helpful to particular children? What are your own issues that interfere consistently with your ability to be helpful? And perhaps most important of all: What can you do to help yourself when you find yourself stuck in conflicts that do not seem to have a satisfactory resolution? In much the same way that we teach people to talk to themselves constructively, to reframe situations in a more positive light, to alter their perceptions and interpretations of situations, counselors as well could benefit from taking their own advice.

Chapter 4 contains a fairly comprehensive catalogue of things that you can do differently with your most difficult students. Rules of engagement are provided, as well as ways to challenge yourself to work in more flexible, creative ways. After all, one definition of a difficult person is simply someone who cooperates in ways that we do not expect or prefer. Flexibility is thus the key to most of the strategies and interventions that are described.

The final chapter deals with the thorny issue of difficult colleagues. The same principles and strategies that have been described throughout the book can be applied as well to those situations in which we find ourselves at odds with our peers. Certainly, unruly children make our lives more difficult than they need to be, but often our principal sources of stress stem from administrators, teachers, parents, and other counselors who do not appreciate our work. This chapter concludes with a review of the major concepts that have been presented.

Acknowledgments

I am grateful to Gracia Alkema, founder and president of Corwin Press, for her great vision, as well as her sensitivity and caring as an editor, in making this series of practical books for school counselors become a reality. After working together on a half dozen books over the last two decades, I am continually amazed at how she has been able to combine the best qualities of a critical editor with those of the most compassionate and intuitive counselor.

JEFFREY A. KOTTLER
Las Vegas, Nevada

About the Author

Jeffrey Kottler is one of the foremost experts in the area of working with difficult children. He has authored 20 books in the fields of counseling and therapy, several of which have been about resolving conflicts in relationships. His latest books on this subject include *Introduction to Therapeutic Counseling* (with Robert Brown, 1996), *The Language of Tears* (1996), *Growing a Therapist* (1995), *Beyond Blame: A New Way of Resolving Conflicts in Relationships* (1994), *The Heart of Healing: Relationships in Therapy* (with Tom Sexton and Susan Whiston, 1994), *Classrooms Under the Influence: Addicted Families/ Addicted Students* (with Richard Powell and Stanley Zehm, 1994, Corwin Press), *The Emerging Professional Counselor: From Dreams to Realities* (with Richard Hazler, 1994), *On Being a Therapist* (2nd ed., 1993), *Teacher as Counselor* (with Ellen Kottler, 1993, Corwin Press), *Advanced Group Leadership* (1993), *On Being a Teacher* (with Stanley Zehm, 1993, Corwin Press), and *Compassionate Therapy: Working With Difficult Clients* (1992).

Kottler is Professor of Education at Texas Tech University, Lubbock. He is the editor of the *Practical Skills for Counselors* series and may be contacted regarding proposals for future titles at Texas Tech University, College of Education, Box 41071, Lubbock, TX 79409-1071 or at kottler@ttu.edu.

1

Who Are Challenging Students?

As counselors, we spend a disproportionate amount of time thinking about a few students who trouble us the most. These are usually children who we find to be resistant, obstructive, belligerent, and uncooperative. Sometimes they are downright hostile, or even violent.

Students get underneath our skin in myriad ways. They challenge our authority. They question our competence, and have us doing the same. They play mind games. Even when they do make small changes, they refuse to acknowledge them, nor will they ever admit that we played a helpful role. They frustrate us to the point where we want to scream, throttle them, or leave the profession altogether.

At a Loss About What to Do

Teachers call on the services of a counselor when they have already exhausted their own resources. We are often the last resort, the final alternative before the child is evicted from school jurisdiction. There we sit, content to catch up on paperwork that has been piling up, and a child appears at the door. He is holding a crumbled-up piece of paper in his fist that vaguely resembles a referral form.

You put on your best empathic face, sport an inviting smile, and ask him to have a seat. He continues standing. With a sigh and visible show of patience, you ask how you can help him. He throws the pink ball of paper into your lap, and then curls his lips into a satisfied smile.

You ask him what's so funny. Barely, just under his breath, you think you hear him say, "Fuck you."

"Excuse me? What did I hear you say?"

[Mumbling] "Nothing important."

"I'd like you to come here for a moment. I think we have some things to discuss."

"I don't think so."

He gets up and walks out of the room, leaving you to stare at the little ball of paper now resting on your desk. Not sure what else to do, you carefully unravel the referral slip filled out meticulously by the student's teacher. It reads: "This student seems to have a problem with authority. Please talk to him before he returns to my class."

Right.

This challenging student just happens to be of a cultural background different from that of the teacher, and you, the counselor. Interestingly, he is not like this in all of his classes, or with all authority figures. In fact, with his music teacher, who is of the same ethnic background, he is one of the most cooperative and motivated students in the class. Clearly, what has transpired between you and the student, as well as between him and his teacher, is not only about unacceptable and inappropriate behavior in need of control but also about cultural gaps between you. There is a noteworthy absence of respect that all of the participants in this conflict—student, teacher, counselor—feel toward one another. Each feels very much like a victim. Furthermore, after this interaction is over, each will receive considerable sympathy from their respective peers as to how misunderstood he or she has been.

In the Eye of the Beholder

Although we might all agree that the student who swore at the counselor or teacher and then stormed out of the room—all without *apparent* provocation—would be a challenging case for almost anyone, such consensus is not always possible in other cases. In fact, there is remarkable diversity among teachers and counselors as to what constitutes a "difficult" student.

Imagine, for example, the following scenario. You are conducting a guidance unit on self-esteem in a classroom. You ask students to take out a paper and pencil to take a pretest on a lesson you are about to present. One student raises her hand. You recognize her, puzzled because you see a look of determination on her face. She asks you, politely but firmly, "May I ask what the purpose of this exercise is?"

How would you interpret this student's behavior?

Of course, this is an unfair question without making other contextual cues available to you—her tone of voice, the previous patterns of her behavior, the responses of her fellow students. Nevertheless, consider your assessment of what you think this question means and how you react, viscerally, to it.

A number of possibilities are articulated by several different counselors:

Counselor A: I think she is challenging me, forcing me to be on the defensive.

Counselor B: She seems to feel a need to exert some control. Maybe she is feeling threatened.

Counselor C: I think she is nervous about the test and is trying to think of a way to postpone it.

Counselor D: I *like* the question. I think that is a reasonable question. It challenges me to provide a rationale for my actions.

Counselor E: I wouldn't think anything at all. I don't have enough information to determine what she is really asking.

Each of these hypotheses is perfectly reasonable. What is most interesting about so-called "difficult" students is that not everyone agrees who they are. Get a group of counselors together to describe

their most challenging students and we would hear quite a variety
of nominations:

- "For me it's the student who is hostile, the one who has a chip
  on his shoulder, and it *is* usually a 'him'."
- "I really struggle with the student who is obviously smart and
  capable but doesn't apply him- or herself, doesn't study at all
  or turn in any work."
- "I don't like the smart-ass, the student who always talks back
  and has to have the last word."
- "I can deal with anyone but the student who is withdrawn. She
  sleeps in the back of the room. Doesn't have any life in her."
- "I don't like students who are passive, without any opinions of
  their own. They are teacher-pleasers, always trying to figure
  out what I want to hear."
- "The student who gives me the most trouble is the one who
  is manipulative and plays mind games. Everything is about
  control."
- "I don't like students who are dishonest. I don't mind if they
  are surly, if they show how they feel. I have trouble with those
  who pretend to feel one thing but show me a smoke screen."

Certainly these comments describe familiar characters in our of-
fices and classrooms. Each of us has struggled, at one time or another,
with students who resemble many of these descriptions. The point
is, however, that what constitutes a challenging student is not the
same for all teachers and counselors. In many cases, it is not just the
students' behavior that makes them difficult in the first place; it is how
we react to what they do. In other words, students do not just come
to us as challenging. Sometimes we make them that way.

Students Who Challenge Us the Most

In spite of the differences of opinion among counselors, we can reach
some consensus as to which students we all consider the most challenging. Basically, they can be grouped into the following categories:

Those who violate rules. Perhaps most common, we must confront students who for one reason or another decide that the boundaries that we have established do not apply to them, universally or selectively. This could be the case because they believe the rules are not just, or that they are not enforced fairly. They may not understand what is expected: Perhaps the rules are not clearly stated, or they do not make sense in the context of the student's culture. Finally, they may enjoy the benefits of not playing by the rules—the power they wield, the attention they receive, the control they feel.

Natasha knows very well that smoking is not tolerated anywhere on school property, much less in the girls' bathroom. It is almost as if she is asking to be caught, defying you and anyone else you can mobilize to stop her from doing something she is determined to do. She has not yet responded to any discipline or strategy you have used. She states clearly that you simply can't make her do anything. You are beginning to believe her.

Those who have given up. Beware of anyone who feels that he or she has nothing left to lose. Some children resort to hostility, even violence, because they do not see other options. They need to exaggerate their power; they believe that the world is a very dangerous place, that others will hurt them if they see any signs of weakness, and that the best way to protect themselves is through intimidation (Roth, 1991).

Generally speaking, we like our students to be fairly articulate; express what they are feeling in honest, sincere, and respectful ways; and be grateful for our best intentions to help them. Children who have given up tend to be either withdrawn and nonresponsive or passionately angry and nonresponsive. In either case, they will not acknowledge our assistance, nor will they cooperate in ways that we would prefer.

Mickey doesn't talk much. But then he does not need to say very much to communicate his utter disdain for you and everything for which you stand. He barely attends to what you are saying, apparently lost in a world of his own that you can't begin to understand. Sometimes he looks at you for a moment in pity, as if you are the one in need of help. Otherwise, he rocks in his chair, humming some tune that begins to grate on your ears. He knows that, of course, and so sings a little louder.

Another kind of student who has given up is the one who is unmotivated. Such children feel little drive to accomplish school-related tasks. In fact, they may be tremendously motivated to do other things at home, in their neighborhoods, or on school grounds, even if such behavior often goes unappreciated by adults.

Felicia, for example, appears to be a lump of clay to her teachers and counselor. She sits quietly in class, sometimes even naps, and rarely speaks to anyone. She has yet to turn in a single homework assignment; when she is asked about this noncompliance, she simply shrugs. She seems fairly bright, from what little you've observed, but her teachers report that even when called on directly in class, she rarely responds. If ever there was an unmotivated child, it is Felicia.

Away from the view of school, however, Felicia is intensely motivated to help her younger sisters. Because her parents are rarely around, the responsibility falls primarily on her to get her siblings dressed in the morning, feed them, entertain them, protect them, and get them places they need to be. Remarkably, she even helps them with their homework, even if she does not do her own. Although Felicia appears to be unmotivated, her lack of commitment is limited mostly to school grounds, not the areas of her life she considers to be most important.

Those who are manipulative. Students often challenge us when they have a hidden agenda. We cannot trust, at face value, what is being presented. A student comes to us with an apparently genuine request for assistance, to which we graciously respond. Then we discover that there is some other agenda at work here, one at which we can only guess. Another student is a master at "working the system." She knows exactly how to get her way, to get administrators, her parents, and other students to do her bidding. Still another manipulative student plays lots of games to keep you at a distance. There is something about you that is perceived as threatening to him, so he does everything he can think of to get you to reject him.

Nyla tells you how much you are helping her. She is so grateful for all that you have done on her behalf. You are puzzled by this: You can't remember that you had done all that much for her. You are also suspicious about her supposed changes: She looks the same to you, and the same negative reports come in from her teachers. When you confront her with this, she acts misunderstood and hurt. When you attempt to deal with these feelings, she takes quite another tack. The more you talk to her, the more confused you feel, unable to sort out what is real for her and what is part of her elaborate game to keep you off balance.

Those who withhold communication. This group includes students who are passive, withdrawn, or otherwise do not communicate fully, at least according to what we usually expect. This challenging student may remain silent almost all the time, speaking only when absolutely forced to do so. Even then, he may answer in monosyllables. This is often not because the student does not have opinions, or is unable to express himself. He may just be a quiet person, or part of a culture in which speaking in a counseling context is not considered appropriate. He may also be depressed, troubled, insecure, or lack confidence.

Then there are those students who restrict the content of what they say. They may ramble a lot, intellectualize about subjects unrelated to the present discussion, or ask rhetorical questions just to hear themselves speak. The challenge with them is not that they do not contribute but that they do so in a way that precludes *meaningful* communication.

Those who are severely impaired. This group includes those children who cannot cooperate with your best efforts to help them because of some underlying organic or physiological problem. This could be the result of an underlying neurological problem, such as an attention deficit disorder or a mental illness, or it could be related to substance abuse. In spite of best intentions to change their behavior, such children demonstrate a degree of impulsivity and erratic conduct that makes it difficult for them to comply with defined norms.

Felipe is an absolutely delightful young man. He is charming, bright, and extremely talented as a musician. He also claims that doing well in school is important to him, although his attendance is inconsistent and he often falls asleep in class. During a few consultations with him, you have found him to be highly motivated and engaging, responsive to your suggestions, and open to honest discussions. You are perplexed, however, about why his behavior has not changed even though he works so well with you during sessions.

Later you learn that he lives at home with his parents, grandmother, and three older siblings, all of whom are alcoholics. Parties rage well into the night. He often partakes in the festivities—staying up late drinking most nights, waking the next morning with a hangover. There is no way that he can attend school on a regular basis and perform successfully as long as he drinks alcohol. No counselor in the world can help him until he abstains from all alcohol or until his home environment is changed.

Those who are "at risk." This term has been applied so generally it can refer to those in imminent danger of child abuse, those who are especially vulnerable to substance abuse, those who are on the verge of leaving school, or even the estimated 80% of children who come from supposedly dysfunctional families (Webb, 1992). For our purposes, we are concerned with those children who are especially likely to develop behaviors disruptive to themselves or others. These are kids who may not yet be identified as challenging or difficult, but for whom there is a great probability that problems may very well develop.

What makes this group of students so challenging for us is that because they have not yet developed problems, the motivation to change anything is minimal. "So what if all my brothers and sisters are drug dealers, and my parents are both heavy users. That shit ain't gonna happen to me."

Those who push your buttons. This last group is actually the most common. It is not solely the students' behavior that we find difficult or challenging but also the feelings and reactions that their actions elicit in us. In other words, some students do not just come to us as obstructive or resistant: We make them that way.

I recall one instance in which a preschool child was initially reluctant to comply with a reasonable request to clean up a mess she had made. There was something about the way she defied me that really started a slow burn. Actually, I do not think she was as much defying me as she was practicing some new assertive skills, and therein lies the problem: I took this little altercation *very* personally. I don't even think that I was seeing her for who she was but rather as another child she reminded me of who had once given me a hard time.

I spoke more caustically to this little girl than I needed to in order to make my point. Bless her heart: In turn, she decided that I was not going to order her around, so she became even more defiant. Before we knew it, we were both involved in a major conflict that could have easily been avoided if I had not overreacted to what I perceived was a challenge to my authority. It was not so much that she was a difficult child as she was a confident young girl who did not take kindly to being spoken to in a disrespectful manner. In all honesty, I made her far more difficult than she would have otherwise been.

Questions to Ask Yourself

Children are difficult not only because of the ways they act but because of how we interpret their behavior. Although there is some consensus about which children are among the most challenging for counselors, it is worthwhile for us to consider situations from other angles. A number of questions might prove helpful in this regard:

- Who experiences the child as difficult?
- How does the child view the situation?
- How does his or her family view things?
- How do his or her best friends view things?
- What precipitates the problem behavior?
- What are the effects of this behavior?
- What would be the consequences of changing the behavior?

- What are some alternative ways to frame the problem?
- What is your (the counselor's) contribution to the conflict?

These questions can help clarify why particular students seem so difficult to counsel by placing their actions in a context that considers the circular causes and effects, as well as your own perceptions of what is happening.

To succeed with challenging cases, it is critical to understand exactly what is going on and why children are acting the way they are. In the next chapter, we examine counseling from two different angles—one that explores the reasons why children act out, and the other that looks at the ways we sometimes make things far more difficult than they need to be.

2

Why Do They Act the Way They Do?

One of the things that makes it difficult for us to deal with so-called challenging students is not understanding why they act the way they do. It seems incomprehensible to us that some children will go to such lengths to make life so difficult, for themselves and for us, when it would be so much easier to be cooperative. Why, for instance, would a student repeatedly neglect to turn in homework assignments which require at most 15 minutes per night, when the consequences involve severe punishment by parents and teachers? Why would a student create a disturbance that she knows is going to get her kicked out of school? Why would someone get in fights that he is certain he is going to lose? Why must students be so unpleasant and unreasonable, when it seems so much easier to get along?

They Are Doing the Best They Can

Before we can ever hope to reach challenging students, we must first understand why they are acting the way they are. All behavior, whether it is comprehensible to you or not, persists because it is helpful in some way to that person: It has some functional value or some protective role in the family.

If the child were not getting something out of the behavior, if it were not serving him or her in some way, the child would do something else. Granted, *what* he is getting may seem mysterious, or even perverse; nevertheless, all behavioral patterns that continue are being reinforced in some way, if not by friends than by some inner reward.

Medical professionals discovered long ago that certain patients recover from surgery far more quickly than others. In some cases, people who should improve rather routinely instead languish in their beds and demonstrate only the slightest improvement, even when there is no medical reason to account for this slow recovery. Apparently, some patients receive "secondary gains" from their behavior. They have good reasons for not getting better sooner. They enjoy the benefits of being in a sick role—the attention they are getting, the excuse to remain helpless, the legitimate reason for not rejoining a life that, in some ways, feels abhorrent. Until nurses and doctors address these underlying reasons for the patients' slow recovery, significant progress remains unlikely.

This same conceptual model may be applied to the school situation if you are interested in understanding the reasons why some of your most uncooperative students are acting in particular ways. Even if this perspective does not suggest alternative methods of intervention, it sure makes it easier to respond objectively, because you will not be taking their behavior personally. Challenging students are not doing anything *to you;* rather, they are just doing their best to help themselves or their families.

Because school counselors are offered such a limited perspective of what is really going on with kids, our knowledge is necessarily incomplete. We hear only what children tell us, what their teachers and parents tell us, or what we see with our own eyes. Often, this is not nearly enough information.

An 11-year-old was referred to me because he had been caught setting off the fire alarm at school. His parents were puzzled, as were his teachers, because prior to this incident he had been a model student. I spent a few sessions with this child that were most productive. He seemed contrite and cooperative. He acknowledged his wrongdoing and promised never to do anything like that again. His grateful parents called and praised my miraculous work.

A few weeks later, the parents called again. I had been so helpful with their 11-year-old that they wondered if I might be willing to see their eldest son as well. At 17, he was a senior in high school and a star on several athletic teams. Lately, his coaches were benching him because of his defiant behavior. This was not only hurting the boy but also the team, which was losing out on his talent.

Again I was surprised at how quickly things proceeded. It took all of three sessions to explore what was going on. The boy admitted he didn't quite know what the problem was, but he was determined to be more cooperative with his coaches. He thanked me for my help and then reported to his parents that he was now much improved.

At this point, I must admit, I was feeling *very* impressed with myself. Ordinarily, I had never been this successful in such a brief period of time with two children who seemed to be presenting such puzzling problems. Nevertheless, I assumed that my counseling skills were just getting better and better.

When this family called again, asking me if I might see their middle son about some fits of rage he was throwing around the house, I readily agreed. By now, I'm sure that you are nodding your head smugly, seeing the pattern that I had missed—these boys were acting out at school and home for some reason that had to do with their family situation. I am ashamed to admit that it was weeks later before it occurred to me to counsel the parents instead of the children. It took all of 5 minutes to discover that this couple was on the verge of divorce. I also learned that as long as one of their children was having trouble, they presented a united, helpful front. Once things calmed down, however, then they would both resort to their usual screaming and threaten to walk out. Unconsciously, there was a conspiracy among their children to take turns developing problems as a way to keep the family intact.

Although this particular pattern became obvious, in many circumstances it is quite difficult for a school counselor to gather enough information to see the larger picture. For this reason, Peeks (1992) advocates a focused-interview approach with parents of the difficult child to determine what sort of interactive pattern is taking place within the family. It is assumed that the child's symptoms actually help the family make some organizational transition. Table 2.1 lists the kinds of problems that the astute school counselor might detect.

Challenging students act in ways that appear disruptive, resistant, and noncompliant to us because of an agenda, often beyond their own awareness, that is fortified by their behavior. Specifically, such students enjoy the following secondary gains from behavior that we label as difficult.

The student feels empowered. If you feel powerless in your life, at the mercy of adults who control your freedom, at the whim of circumstances that seem grim and without hope, what better way to maintain a sense of personal control than to disrupt the balance of a teacher?

Teachers and counselors are godlings. We are the ones with the authority to decide what goes on within our domain, even who gets to go to the restroom. According to our preferences and moods, we determine who goes to the blackboard, who gets to speak, and what happens when someone does something that we do not like. Just imagine how powerful indeed a child must feel if he or she can get to us, really get underneath our skin. Sure, there are some nasty side effects to making a teacher mad, but for those who perceive they have nothing to lose, a censure or trip to the principal's office is a small price to pay.

Students who revel in their disruptive power are living in a culture in which such nihilistic acts are respected, if not reinforced. As one student describes this attitude: "Yeah, I'm in trouble a lot. So what? No big deal. I'd rather destroy things on my own terms than be a victim of someone else, especially a teacher. I mean I can't talk back to my father or he'd kill me; he probably would. I can't fight with my friends too much or they won't have anything to do with me. But a teacher? What can *you* do? Kick me out of your room? So what? It

TABLE 2.1 Home-Life Factors That Can Exacerbate In-School
Problems for Students

Disasters	*Transitions*
Natural disasters (e.g., floods, earthquakes)	Family development (e.g., child leaving home)
Financial or legal problems	Individual development
Tragedies (e.g., death, victimization)	Reorganization following divorce or remarriage
Organizational Disputes	*Hierarchical Disorder*
Disagreements with school	Intrusive grandparents
Problems with community agencies	Unhealthy family coalitions
Distractions from other family problems	Unequal parental power
Discipline	*Marital Conflict*
Lack of parental consensus	Ongoing tension and conflict
Lack of boundaries and clear rules	Covert battles with children in middle
Inconsistent enforcement	Imminent divorce

makes me feel good to think that I can make you miserable right
along with me."

Perverse reasoning? Certainly. Counterproductive if your priority
is learning? Assuredly so. However, if your intention is to feel
powerful, if you are part of a culture that sees teacher–authority types
as part of the mainstream establishment that seeks to dominate and
control people like you, there is tremendous satisfaction in getting
your licks in while you can.

The student enjoys attention. Ask a student why she keeps being so
uncooperative and, if she were honest, she might tell you, "Because
it's fun!" Indeed it *is* fun, in a way, to enjoy the attention of your
peers. If you can't win this spotlight in other ways, say through

your athletic prowess or academic achievement or fancy clothes, stirring things up in class is not a bad option.

In the culture of some students, there is much to be gained from drawing any attention to yourself. As comedian and ex–class clown George Carlin explained in one of his routines: If he wasn't learning much of value in school, why not deprive others of their education? He could not make it as a scholar or a football player, but boy, could he make kids laugh.

The student avoids responsibility for his or her behavior. Some students are threatened by our attempts to reach out to them. Even if they wanted to excel in their schoolwork, their peer and sometimes family cultures would sabotage their efforts. They feel much ambivalence. On the one hand, they may find us engaging on a personal level and feel intrigued by things we are doing in class. On the other hand, if they let themselves be drawn in by us, if they were to cooperate with our plans, they would lose status in their other culture, which is far more important.

One student explains, "I once brought schoolwork home to do and everyone made fun of me. My friends thought I'd totally lost it. My mom did not like the idea that I might be smarter than her. My brother and sisters teased me. Forget it. No way I could do any work at home."

The scenario unfolds in which the student tests the counselor in some way—becomes challenging, refuses to cooperate, or otherwise draws attention in distracting ways. The counselor has no choice but to intervene. The student then feels misunderstood and unfairly treated. Furthermore, the counselor is blamed for the problems: "Hey, why should I put up with this crap? I never get a break."

The payoff to this way of thinking is that the student is not at fault for the troubles. In addition, such a strategy keeps the counselor from getting too close.

The student is able to maintain the status quo and ward off perceived threats. As is implied from the previous secondary gain, the student may seek to distract the counselor. This is a recurrence of the theme of destroying things on your own terms: "If you really knew me, you would probably reject me. I am rejecting you first, though, so you can't hurt me."

A predictable sequence of events ensues: (a) The counselor reaches out to the student; (b) the student feels threatened by the overture and so withdraws; (c) the counselor feels rebuffed and so backs off; (d) the student acts provocatively to regain attention on his or her own terms; (e) the counselor steps in to set limits; (f) the student feels victimized and misunderstood, escalating the disruptive behavior; (g) the counselor increases the levels of attempted control. And so on. The conflict eventually reaches the point where both parties feel misunderstood.

The teacher or counselor thinks, "Why should I even try with these kids? I have done everything I can to reach out to this child and all he has done is try to hurt me."

The student thinks, "All of these people are alike. I knew I shouldn't trust any of them. First she gets on my case and starts nagging me. Then when I try to be myself more she cuts me off. No sense in even trying."

Neither counselor nor student has the foggiest idea about what the other person is all about. Each of them feels justified in writing the other one off.

It is by understanding these underlying dynamics of the challenging student's behavior, as well as the larger context of his or her family and peer culture, that effective efforts to be helpful are possible. Until you can answer the question "What exactly is this student getting out of this behavior?" interventions are likely to be misguided. This is only the first step in trying to work through conflicts with challenging students.

Additional Functions of Conflict

Given the headaches and heartaches that we normally associate with conflict, whether it is with a student, colleague, or family member, we do not often consider how such interpersonal skirmishes provide a number of benefits—not only for students who may be the initiators of the disagreement, but also for those of us who exacerbate the problems for reasons of our own. Before you react defensively—"What, me? How dare you suggest that I do anything to keep conflicts going; I certainly have enough to worry about that I don't need to make matters worse!"—I'd like you to consider some of the positive things that can result from conflict.

Releases tension. When tempers are flaring, emotional energy is being expressed. There is an intensity to conflict in which both participants are discharging pent-up feelings. One counselor explains this reaction:

> I don't like one of the other guys I have to work with. He is pushy. He always tries to boss me around. Even worse, he doesn't really know what he is doing and I'm already cleaning up after him, covering for his mistakes.
>
> There are many times that I would really like to tell him off, put him in his place, but I never do. I just swallow my frustration and go about my work. So there I am feeling angry as hell, and in walks this student with a note telling me that I'm supposed to fix his behavior or something. The kid mouths off to me, but I've had just about enough for the day: I give it right back to him. Before we know it, we are both yelling at each other. I don't know if he felt any better afterwards, but I sure did!
>
> We both blew off a little steam and then we were able to sit down and figure out something to do. I apologized first, and then that made it easier for him to tell me that he was sorry too. It was actually a great way to start, although I certainly would never have planned it that way.

Maintains distance. Another function that conflict serves is to control how just how close one will let him- or herself get to others, psychologically speaking. Some children, who are not used to being involved with adults as compassionate and caring as we are, feel vulnerable and confused by their feelings. They have little experience in such healthy relationships and feel unprepared to deal with them.

One of the most effective and efficient ways to push away a well-meaning teacher or counselor is to create some sort of dramatic conflict. For example, I recall one 4-year-old with whom I had been working to help control her temper tantrums. She loved our sessions together because I was one of the few adults in her life who responded to her consistently. There were certain aspects of her behavior that I would not tolerate, but I was always calm and caring in the ways that I would restrain her, never raising my voice. Over time, we came to care about one another very much, and this frightened her.

Every few weeks or so, she would deliberately provoke some argument. She would refuse to abide by the rules we had established. She would do something that she knew would upset me. At first, I wondered why she would deliberately try to upset me, until I realized that in her own ingenious way she was keeping me from getting closer to her than she could handle.

Highlights issues of control. In one way or another, conflict usually ends up being about who is going to get his or her way. Disagreements thus signal that both parties are trying their best to exert some sort of power over the other.

The counselor wants the student to abide by rules that she believes are important; the student has his own agenda—to be given the freedom to do things the way he prefers. The conflict between them is the inevitable result of two people determined to get their way. For reasons mentioned earlier, the student actually enjoys the conflict, with the accompanying feelings of power; he feels little motivation to resolve things satisfactorily. He may not be getting his way exactly but he is also keeping the counselor from getting her way as well. Although not an ideal solution, it certainly creates a respectable impasse for those who are not used to getting their way very often.

Underscores underlying issues to be resolved. Conflicts get our attention. They are disagreeable experiences that churn up a number of negative feelings. As such, they act as motivators to resolve whatever is really disturbing to people.

A counselor was about halfway through a parent conference, going through the usual spiel about how their daughter's low achievement was more a reflection of poor motivation rather than lack of ability, when the father and mother erupted into a dispute about whose fault it was that their child was a failure. Interestingly, however, they didn't actually talk about their daughter but about whose turn it was to pick up groceries on the way home. The counselor, caught in the middle, felt like he was watching a tennis match, so well rehearsed were their respective "shots" at one another. During an opportune pause in the argument, he offered that perhaps what they were really upset about was how powerless they felt to change their child's behavior. Their conflict only drew attention to the degree of their helplessness and frustration.

Creating Difficult Students

Counselors encounter difficulties that are caused by their own actions (or inactions) under the following circumstances:

When we are missing information. A student may appear to be unusually reticent and resistant to our best efforts to be helpful. Then we learn that she has been betrayed before by someone she trusted. Further, we learn that one of the messages she received growing up was not to trust *anyone* in a helping role.

When we hold invalid assumptions. We assume that a child has a problem with authority. After all, in response to our most innocuous requests for compliance we encounter marked stubbornness. This assumption is challenged after discovering that what appears to be hostility to authority is actually quite a sensible defense against further physical and sexual abuse that she suffers at home.

When we don't do something very well. There are times when, as a result of something we say or do, we create difficulties where none previously existed. When we fail to provide adequate structure or clear enough instructions, or when we ask students do to things that are beyond their capability, we create frustration that leads to other undesirable side effects. When we cut a student off or censure someone, or otherwise show behavior that is *perceived* as disrespectful, we may have created a difficult student. When we bungle a confrontation, misread cues, or embarrass a student through the best of intentions, we may have created an enemy, or at least someone who no longer feels cooperative toward us.

The problem is not in making mistakes, which are inevitable. Students give us the benefit of the doubt when they know we are trying our hardest to understand them and treat them fairly. They are especially forgiving when we can acknowledge our errors and misjudgments. Nevertheless, we spend an awful lot of time complaining to one another about how awful certain students are without looking at our contributions to the conflicts. The question we should be asking is not "What is wrong with this challenging student?" but "What might we have done to exacerbate these difficulties?"

Just as students can be labeled difficult, so too can counselors. In one sense, perhaps there are no difficult students. After all, that is simply a judgment on the part of a teacher about behavior that is misunderstood. Even the most belligerent child is acting in a particular way because he or she is getting something useful from such behavior.

In Summary

We hear teachers, parents, principals, and other counselors say all the time, "I just don't know what's wrong with these kids today. What makes them act so badly?" Of course, in their own discussions when they are left alone, children ask themselves the same question about adults—how can we be so stupid and out of it?

There is a simple answer to why so-called difficult children act the way they do: It works for them. We may feel angry and indignant because their behavior seems unreasonable and dysfunctional, but that is only because we aren't looking at things from their viewpoint—which is they are just doing the best they can. If they knew how to do something else that worked better for them, they would do that instead.

Of course, our job is to teach them more socially appropriate alternatives. To do that, however, requires us first to understand why they act as they do, or what they are getting out of those strategies. Second, and just as important, we must examine not only their behaviors, motives, and internal reactions, but our own as well. Conflict, after all, always involves the contributions of two parties who are both acting stubbornly.

3

How Do They Get Underneath Your Skin?

Your worst nightmare walks in the door. This child gets to you like fingernails scraping a blackboard, like a piece of spinach caught between your teeth, like a dull ache that won't go away. Furthermore, you have no choice but to work with this student; there is no other option. Who is this student?

Each of us has a secret list of students we consider most difficult—a list based not so much on what they do as on the ways we react to their behavior. Something gets in the way of our feeling particularly empathic and caring toward them. We feel ourselves becoming impatient, rigid, argumentative, even unreasonable with them in ways we never would with anyone else. We spend an inordinate amount of time thinking about these children, much of it unproductive. We whine and complain to colleagues, family members, and anyone else who will listen, about how tough we have it. We tell "war stories" about the latest battles that we have fought to a standstill. Furthermore, if we were totally honest, we would have to admit that there is just something about them that rubs us the wrong way.

Those Who Don't "Fight Fair"

Although some students become challenging for us to work with because of our issues as much as theirs, some of them earn the label *resistant* through their own hard work. These are the dilemmas we face when involved with someone who will not "fight fair," who resorts to sometimes ingenious strategies that appear cooperative but who actually is doing everything possible, consciously or not, to sabotage things.

I remember seeing one such individual in counseling. I assume she was referred to me in the first place because other people in her life were banging their heads against walls in frustration. For the longest time I could not figure out what Candy's problem was. Here was a young woman who presented herself as the prototype of the perfect client—she was sugary sweet, appeared extremely cooperative, would do most anything I asked of her, and was effusive in her gratitude about how much I was helping her. The only problem was that although she was a model citizen in my office, Candy was a skilled provocateur in the jungles of her own world.

When I confronted her about this discrepancy, she decided to turn her able talents to make my life as miserable as her own. Because she deduced quite accurately that helplessness was the key to getting underneath my skin, she expressed her tremendous rage toward the world and anger toward me by developing almost every set of symptoms I had ever read about. Then she would call me late at night and beg for help. Or she would have car trouble on the way to an appointment in which she was to report significant changes in her life. Sometimes she would just sit in my office, perfectly still, tears rolling down her face, and refuse to say a single word for the hour.

When I interpreted her behavior as unexpressed anger, Candy "punished" me by skipping the next two sessions altogether. When

I confronted her on that passive-aggressive ploy, she sweetly acknowledged there might be some merit to the point ("Oh, Dr. Kottler, sometimes you say the most insightful things"), bided her time, and then ambushed me later by checking herself into the hospital. Candy asked that I apologize to her for being so mean before she would agree to comply with her treatment. And although over a period of years, with patience, compassion, and firm limit setting, she did improve significantly, she never once admitted that there was anything deliberate about her manipulative ploys.

Remember now, Candy and people just like her are walking around in the world. Younger versions of her are in your school as students. Because they feel so little power in their lives, they get a visceral thrill out of controlling your life as much as possible. Although few of the people you ever meet will manifest such extreme manipulative behavior and such severe emotional disturbance as Candy, most of us have encountered on more than a few occasions attempts by people to control us through manipulative gestures.

The main challenge in dealing with these people is that unless they are willing to fight fair—that is, to acknowledge their hostile feelings and express them appropriately—there is little we can do to help them. That is why it is useless to try to change them or blame them: You will only escalate the struggle. Instead, direct your attention toward three priorities that will be discussed in this and later chapters. First (and most important): Protect yourself from collateral damage that results from their self-destructive ploys. Second: Control what you do inside your own head so that you do not hurt yourself with remorse and blame. And third: Diagnose accurately which manipulative strategy is being used, and respond with an appropriate counterresponse—not just externally, but internally as well.

Protecting Yourself

Sigmund Freud was the first to suggest to counselors that a stance of neutral detachment is most helpful for maintaining enough distance from people who are acting out. His use of the couch in treatment, for example, was invented as much for his own comfort as it was to facilitate free association. Being able to sit outside of his clients' line of vision allowed him to remain more objective and out of the direct onslaught of their anger or frustration.

Detachment, which is essential to psychoanalytic relationships, is also helpful in other conflicted interactions. Taking a step back allows us to disengage from the personal aspects of a conflict and remain clear enough to decide how to respond effectively without being distracted by our feelings of hurt and anger.

Note, for example, in the following heated interaction between myself and a client who was particularly obstructive and accusatory in his style, how I attempted to keep myself from getting sucked into the vortex of his anger:

Client:	How the hell can you live with yourself knowing you are such a fraud?
Me:	You seem particularly angry at me today, even more than usual. *(That's right. Keep the ball in his court.)*
Client:	There you go again with those shrink games. You must think I'm awfully stupid.
Me:	*(Got me. Or I should say he is getting himself. This really isn't about me.)* I am not playing games with you. I just notice that as long as you keep the focus on me, you don't have to deal with your own issues. *(There. That sounds right.)*
Client:	Very clever. You don't know what you are doing or how to help me, but you keep seeing me anyway.
Me:	*(He's probably right about that.)* You want me to give you a guarantee? *(Oops. He is getting to me. Now I am being defensive. Take a deep breath. Back off.)* You seem awfully disappointed in me and what I've been able to do for you, but also disappointed in yourself. There is a lot at stake for you in this relationship. *(Much better. In order to help him, I've got to stay calm.)*
Client:	Look, we can go around and around about this forever. Since I am the client here, I would just as soon talk about why you can't help me.

Me:	*(He is tapping into my own doubts about my work. Sensitive soul that he is, he knows I wonder about whether I am really doing anything as a counselor.)* If you don't feel that you are getting help from me, perhaps you'd like to see someone else? *(Damn! He got me. Now I am really defensive.)*
Client:	Not so fast. You think you can drop me just because I'm giving you a hard time? What's the matter? Can't you stand the heat?

If I'm ever to help this person in pain it is imperative that I not allow myself to become emotionally threatened to the point where I start defending myself or attacking in retribution. This is, naturally, very difficult to do when the other person is as skilled as this student at finding vulnerable areas to exploit. On the other hand, it is often helpful to realize that the reason people are referred to us in the first place is because they are having trouble coping with others. In a sense, it is their "job" as a client to engage in the same self-defeating strategies with us as they do with others. Unless they are willing to reveal their true (but often infuriating) selves to us, we cannot really help them.

Pushing Our Buttons

Each of us has unresolved issues that are constantly coming to the surface at inopportune times. Most of us actually entered the counseling field for reasons other than pure altruism. Yes, we enjoy helping people and making the world a better place, but we are also seeking to save ourselves in the process.

Some of the buttons that are pushed by certain students include the following:

- Our fear of failure
- Our secret feelings of incompetence, of being a fraud
- Our feelings of helplessness, ineptitude, and impotence when we cannot fix things and make them better
- Our memories of the most painful times of our own childhood
- Our own need for control

During those times when students do or say things that force us to look at our sore spots, or relive unresolved issues related to control, power, and authority, we react or, more likely, *overreact* to what is happening. What starts out as a little disagreement becomes a full-fledged battle of wills.

I know, for example, that I have great trouble with anger. When I was a kid, my parents fought a lot, and I did everything I could to hide from the emotional hurricanes that would hit my house at regular intervals. I pride myself on the control I have shown throughout my life to neither acknowledge nor express anger. When anyone acts angry toward me, I either pout or, if possible, get as far away as I can.

In my work with preschoolers, adolescents, and graduate students, I have inevitably encountered individuals who, at times, feel anger— toward themselves, toward classmates, and, most painfully, toward me. During those times when a student has become enraged, or even just a little angry, I have not always responded in my best (or professionally appropriate) manner. In some cases, if I had just let things run their course or shown some understanding of what the person might have been feeling, the situation would have resolved itself. Instead, because I felt so defensive and wounded by displays of anger, my tendency was often to quickly cut the student off. I have noticed time and time again that this was a turning point when an otherwise responsive student became challenging for me to deal with thereafter. To put it another way: We became difficult for one another because the relationship irrevocably changed. The part that is most difficult for me to own is that this student did not start out being resistant to me and what we were doing in class or sessions: I helped to make the person that way by how I reacted to his or her behavior.

How do you know when a student has gotten underneath your skin?

- When you spend an inordinate amount of time thinking about a particular child, or complaining about him or her to others
- When you repeatedly find yourself misunderstanding a child, and feeling misunderstood yourself by him or her

- When you are aware of feeling particularly frustrated, helpless, and blocked with a child
- When your empathy and compassion are compromised and you find it difficult to feel respectful and caring toward a child

Each of these symptoms may signal that you have lost your composure and objectivity, that your own unresolved issues may be getting in the way of being truly helpful to a particular student. Therefore, if we are going to talk about so-called difficult clients, we would be negligent if we downplayed our own tendencies to become difficult counselors. Where should you look for such vulnerable spots? The following are a few of the most common ones.

Seeing ourselves mirrored. There is no doubt that one of the most painful aspects of working with children—whether as a parent, teacher, or counselor—is that we must relive our own childhood over and over again. We see things every day that remind us of our own experiences in school. Sometimes we even see ourselves in the vision of a particular child.

When we experience students as being especially difficult, sometimes we are responding not just to who they are in the present but also who they remind us of. This, after all, is the hallmark of what psychoanalysts describe as countertransference, that distorted reaction that alters our perception of reality. Instead of seeing particular students as they are, we see ourselves or someone else they bring to mind. Let's face it—every kid we see reminds us of another one we have encountered before.

A reality check permits us to consider whether the extent to which a child appears to be difficult is really just our own exaggerated response to a distorted image. Of course, it takes an extraordinary amount of personal clarity and honest self-reflection to recognize this pattern. One counselor, for example, was finding himself especially annoyed with a third-grade bully who was terrorizing some of the other children. Rather than feel the least compassion or empathy for this child, the counselor was overidentifying with the victims to the extent that he kept trying to exact revenge, not only for the bully's present behavior but for all the bullying the counselor had ever suffered in his own life.

Some professionals would say that identifying this distortion and then counteracting it is very difficult, if not impossible, without years of intensive therapy and continual weekly supervision that is geared toward recognizing countertransference issues as they emerge. Nevertheless, most of us are aware of primary personal issues that we have not yet fully resolved, even if we aren't yet prepared to work through them.

Haunted by the past. So, where are *you* most vulnerable? What are the major problems with which you have struggled throughout your life? Which patterns in your most conflicted relationships tend to repeat themselves again and again?

In my experience, it might be helpful to look at the extent to which you have fully resolved the following issues, most or all of which seem to be common for counselors:

- *Intimacy.* To what extent have you been able to create healthy, intimate relationships in your life? When you feel needy or stifled in other relationships, it is not unusual that such dynamics also play out in your sessions with clients.
- *Approval.* How well do you deal with things when other people do not give you the validation that you would prefer? You may find yourself doing things in sessions that have little to do with helping anyone other than yourself.
- *Power.* How well do you handle struggles when another person seeks to control you? Some client relationships become ridden with conflict primarily because we persist in establishing that we are the ones in charge, even at the expense of reaching identified therapeutic goals.

These are just a few of the hundreds of themes that play themselves out in our sessions every day. We are tested constantly— pushed to examine those issues that are often the most frightening for us to consider. And one theme to which I referred earlier can be particularly annoying and distressful.

It is one of our deepest, darkest secrets that most of us feel like frauds. Much of the time, we do not really know what we are doing in our work—we are improvising, sometimes even faking it. We don't know nearly as much as we pretend to know, nor can we always apply our preferred interventions with the deftness and fluency we would like. During moments of honest self-reflection, we also admit that sometimes our primary motive is not to succeed but to *avoid failure.*

No matter how many people you have helped before, here sits this resistant child who will not respond to anything you do. She is a dramatic reminder of the limits of what you can do. She mocks you, not so much by her taunting but by her stubborn refusal to get better. A quiet but painful whisper in your head reminds you that you may have lost your magic. Maybe you cannot help her. Maybe you can't help anyone.

As long as the student stays stuck, you feel like a failure. Surely someone brighter and more capable than you would know exactly what to do with this case. If only you had a doctorate, or had attended one more workshop, or had read a few more books, you would be able to help this person.

You shake your head, as if to clear your mind, and then say all the right things that you have heard before. There are limits to what you can do. It is the student's job to change. You are taking too much responsibility for the outcome of this case; you are overinvested. Yes, you nod your head—this is all true. But you still feel like a failure. You look at this kid, and she reminds you of how helpless and powerless you feel much of the time, despite your effective facade.

Engaging the Challenging Student

When counselors are stuck, the first place they like to start is with the student. During attempts at consultation or supervision, the counselor wants to talk about what the student is doing, or not doing, or what can be done to change the student's attitudes and behavior. I have quite a different strategy in mind, one that starts with your own behavior first.

Whenever you feel at an impasse in your relationships with students (or anyone else for that matter), I suggest that you begin with yourself by asking the following questions:

What personal issues of yours are being triggered by this encounter? More likely than not, the student is challenging your sense of competence.

What expectations are you demanding of this student? Often students act out because they are either unwilling or unable to do what you want. It may be time to reassess what you are asking and make changes in light of what might be more reasonable or realistic.

What are you doing to create or exacerbate the problems? Look at your need for control and the ways you respond when you feel this control is being challenged. Are you pushing this student in ways that are designed to be genuinely helpful to him or her, or are such designs ultimately of more help to you?

Who does this challenging child remind you of? To what extent might you be distorting what is going on with this student? In what ways might you be responding not to who he or she really is but who you imagine the student to be, based on prior experiences with others?

Which of your needs are not being met? It is not pleasant to admit that you have certain personal needs in your work—that students not only learn but feel grateful to you for your help, that they show appropriate deference, that they confirm your favorite theories about the way people should act, and that they laugh at your jokes.

The intent of questions such as this is to help you to examine thoroughly and honestly your own internal reactions to what is taking place. When you are stuck in a conflicted relationship, rather than blame the student for being a particular way (about which you can do little), look first at what you might be doing to magnify the difficulties. Change born of self-reflection is actually far easier to effect because it is within your control.

How Can You Help Yourself?

No matter how many resources are available to help you with difficult students, there are still limits to what you can do. You are well aware that there are children who are not going to improve no matter what you or anyone else may do. They live in home environments that are so toxic that they are likely to be scarred for life. They have suffered traumas from which they will need years to recover—far longer than the meager time that you have to work with them. They show the early signs of what we recognize as personality disorders that impair their ability to engage in healthy relationships. Or they are simply stubborn young people who are determined to make life miserable for themselves, and anyone else they can capture in their web.

We also have to accept the fact that we just cannot help everyone we would like to, not just because of their limitations but because of our own. Each of us tends to work well with some kinds of people and not so well with others. We all have our sore spots, our areas of weakness. These include deficiencies in our skills. Some of us are better at confronting or interpreting or role-playing than others. One counselor is especially effective in working with passive, withdrawn girls. Another has particular success doing groups but not with individual sessions. Still another counselor works miracles in the classroom when presenting self-esteem units but is not nearly as effective working one-on-one.

No matter how much we know and can do, or how much experience we have had, we still have to accept the reality that no matter how hard we try, we cannot reach everyone. Under such circumstances, or whenever it appears that a positive outcome is not likely in spite of our best intentions and more inventive strategies, we would be well-advised to work on ourselves as well as our students.

Isn't this, after all, what we tell people over and over again? You cannot change other people—you can only change yourself. Counselors sometimes feel exempt from this premise. We feel special because of our training. We believe that we really can save children, get them to turn things around even though they may not even have an interest in doing so. Sure enough, this strong belief in our own powers to heal really can work miracles! Often, we are indeed able to get through to the most defiant children who refused to cooperate. But sometimes we must accept the limits of what is within our control. Under such circumstances, there is work we can do with ourselves (sometimes with a little help from a friend) to deal with unsatisfactory outcomes and irreconcilable conflicts.

Don't Take the Conflict Personally

Some counselors have the propensity not so much to blame others for their problems but instead place the full burden of responsibility on themselves. I, for one, can be guilty of just such tendencies. I would much prefer feeling that I am the one at fault for an impasse than the other person. By doing so, I feel powerful—that I have far more influence and control than is actually possible. This way I get to delude myself that there is always something that I can do to get myself out of a sticky situation. I much prefer this level of distortion than feeling helpless because I am being poorly treated without my consent or participation.

Often, counselors like me need reminders that when students are being difficult it is not so much something they are doing to us as what they are doing to themselves. Their acting out may not be directed toward us at all, but rather toward that for which we are a reminder or symbol. We know all this intellectually, of course. It is interesting, however, how often we forget about this simple idea of transference when we persist in personalizing everything.

Time and again, when we become indignant or angry or feel unappreciated, abused, or misunderstood, it is because we are telling ourselves that this difficult child is making our lives miserable. It is as if such children stay up late at night plotting ways to get to us the following day. During moments of grand delusion, I even wonder if there might be a secret association for such people, the Association of Difficult Students, wherein they trade their favorite resistant methods, coach one another in ingenious strategies to stymie their counselors, and even exchange information on which of our soft spots to exploit. It certainly feels that way some days when we face children who seem to be playing us like a virtuoso.

There are few things more helpful under such circumstances than reminding ourselves to stay calm, especially telling ourselves that what is going on is not personal. This is just business. The difficult student is doing his or her best to keep you off balance so you don't get too close. However much you do not like it, remember that he or she is not trying to get you as a person—even though it often feels that way.

It Comes With the Territory

The staff lounge is a dangerous place to hang out because teachers and counselors spend so much time complaining about how poorly they are being treated. "These kids are so ungrateful!" "Let me tell you what this one little boy did to me today." "You think you've got it bad? Let me tell you what happened to me today." And so on.

It sort of reminds me of the absurdity of staff members who work in the complaints department of a company getting together to whine about how people are always complaining to them. Jeez! It's their job to listen to complaints! If they object to those sorts of interactions, they should work somewhere else.

The same holds true for the job of being a school counselor. In a sense, difficult children come with the territory—that's why they are being sent to us in the first place! It is senseless to complain about kids who aren't cooperating when those are exactly the people we have been prepared to help. These children do not yet know how to act any other way.

When we remind ourselves that our role in life is to work with people with whom others are having troublesome dealings, we realize the senselessness of complaining about how tough we have it. It is far easier to respond to such children with compassion, neutrality, and inner calmness when we realize that is exactly what we are trained and paid to do. If we do not like working with difficult children, then perhaps we should think about finding another line of work. And as an aside, if we think that school counselors have it tough, what about those practitioners who work in mental health and hospital settings with the *really* difficult cases?

4

What Can You Do Differently?

Before any intervention, discipline strategy, or helping skill is likely to be helpful, you must first be engaged with the student in such a way that you both feel respected and heard. No student is going to feel grateful or responsive to finger-pointing in which you attempt to blame the student for *your* discomfort with his or her behavior.

In this chapter, I provide some specific suggestions as to what you can do during those times when you are at an impasse with a particular student, when your favorite strategies are not working and you feel at a loss about where to go next.

Some Rules of Engagement

In the interest of resolving disputes with children you find challenging, several suggestions are offered. All of them are intended to be tried within the context of a constructive relationship that is built upon the solid foundation of trust, safety, and respect. Remember, too, that the ideal counseling relationship will continually change according to the particular needs of the client, the stage in the process, and the kind of presenting complaint (Kottler, Sexton, & Whiston, 1994).

Consider, for example, the needy child. This is someone who wants more than we can give, usually to make up for long-term neglect or abuse suffered throughout life. In working with developmentally deprived children, Willison and Masson (1990) found that most often school counselors adopt a parenting role in their attempts to provide the nurturance and support that has rarely been offered. Specifically, this means

1. Demonstrating love and affection
2. Creating a trusting relationship through brief multiple contacts over time
3. Providing a solid "holding environment," one in which firm limits are in place and promised consequences are delivered consistently
4. Offering constructive feedback regarding ways the child could better meet his or her own needs, or at least get them met in more socially appropriate ways
5. Presenting a figure as a benign authority who is dependable
6. Serving as an advocate for the child in negotiations with others
7. Teaching the child coping skills that are not currently part of his or her repertoire

Of course, these guidelines could be applied to work with *any* student, regardless of whether he or she is especially needy or not. The same is true with any of these other rules of engagement.

Detachment without withdrawal. I mentioned previously that there are times when taking a step back from the situation is helpful in reducing your level of perceived personal threat. The hard part is doing this without appearing or feeling punitive: "Okay, forget it! You don't care about all I am trying to do to help you, so I will just leave you to wallow alone."

The object of this position is not to disengage but to create needed therapeutic distance when you are overinvolved. It is important to monitor closely the type and intensity of your engagement with a challenging student. Adjust your distance and involvement to a level where you protect yourself from hurt but also maintain your caring and compassion.

Talk to yourself. Mantras are used by meditators as a way to calm their breathing and maintain a sense of inner tranquility. Usually, you repeat a single word or syllable to yourself over and over again to distract you from intrusions and focus your concentration on the single task of staying relaxed.

In a similar vein, there are longer mantras that can be used during times of stress, especially in those situations where you find yourself locking horns with an obstinate student. The following are some helpful examples:

> *"This isn't personal. This isn't personal. This isn't . . ."* In other words, this saying is a reminder that students are not trying to get you but merely help themselves in the only way they know.
>
> *"He is doing the best he can. He is doing the best . . ."* If this child knew how to do anything else other than what she is doing, she would do it. She is trying to get along as best as she can in a world that has not provided her with many options. She is acting this way because it has worked for her before in the past. Just because you do not like it doesn't mean she must immediately stop.
>
> *"In 100 years this won't matter. In 100 years . . ."* In other words, this is a reminder to keep your perspective on things. What you are so upset about now is partially the result of blowing things out of proportion. This particular skirmish is an insignificant part of your day and life. It does not pollute the other positive things you are doing. It is only a minor annoyance

and inconvenience, hardly a catastrophe. In 100 years, not only will you no longer remember or care about this particular incident, but neither will anyone else.

"Think like an anthropologist. Think . . ." This is a reminder to apply what you know about cultural differences. Take a deep breath and a step back, and try to look at this situation more objectively. How is what the student doing a reflection of her cultural learnings?

This is but a sampling of possibilities. You have likely developed a few of your own mantras that help you during times of stress.

Stop complaining. I referred earlier to how counterproductive it can be to hang out in the teachers lounge with those who are disenfranchised. Sitting around complaining and whining about how awful students are and how they don't care will win you sympathy for a minute or two; after that, you will just continue to feel like a victim. In addition, complaining to family and friends about how tough you've got it only continues to reinforce the idea that students are trying to make your life miserable. That is ridiculous; they are only trying to amuse and protect themselves.

Rather than complain about your challenging students, try an experiment: Pick out one or two positive features about them and make it a point to discuss *those* qualities with colleagues and friends.

Keep your sense of humor. There is no excuse for the line: "I just don't know why kids act the way they do." Sure you do. Because it is fun. If you were to step back and not take their behavior personally, you would recognize as comical the lengths to which some students will go to entertain themselves. One counselor keeps a catalogue of all the antics she sees displayed in her office and classes. When someone comes up with an inventive variation of a new sound, projectile, or method of resistance, she actually feels excited at the prospect of recording it in her journal.

Of course, we cannot laugh out loud as often as we would like when we see students doing the weird and funny things they do. That is not to say, however, that we can't appreciate the creativity and humor of the gesture. Such a posture lightens things up considerably, reminding us that oftentimes this is a game, and not one to be taken all that seriously compared with the things that really matter.

Reframe resistance. Here is a strategy popular among therapists: When you cannot do much with the presenting problem as it is originally labeled, rename it in such a way that you can be helpful. For example, the very idea of "disobedience" is discouraging. The implications are that this student is defying you, and that now you must do something to ensure compliance. Instead, disobedience can be reframed as a form of "creative cooperation." This student is cooperating with you but simply in an unusual way. Such a redefinition of the problem suggests a different set of solutions.

Katrina was constantly drawing attention to herself in class. She was a master of animal sounds. Even more impressive, she could mimic bird calls without seeming to move her lips, so it was very difficult to catch her in the act.

The teacher attempted to restrain this "disruptive behavior" in every way that he could imagine, all to no avail. During a moment of inspiration, he decided to reframe this behavior not as "challenging" or "disruptive" but as "clownish." This young student was simply being a clown, a court jester. Henceforth, the teacher was able to smile as a first reaction to her "Bawdy Parrot" (one of her best) rather than feel challenged and enraged. Within the culture of her family, he knew that this is the way she had always been able to distract her father and keep him from hurting her during his drunken bouts. In the culture of her peers, he realized that she enjoyed tremendous status because of her unusual talents.

The teacher called the student in for a conference, telling her that he greatly admired her skills as a clown. He then suggested, however, that she was performing for the wrong audience because surely they did not give her the full attention she deserved. He offered to set aside some special class time to have her demonstrate her various comic skills; he figured that perhaps she would then no longer need to mimic birds during work time in class.

The point is not whether this particular suggestion worked with the student or not. Whether she changed her behavior in accordance with the reframe was less important than the teacher's being able to view her behavior as less threatening and more amusing. He was far more likely to discover some way to curtail her behavior, or at least harness it, now that he was less emotionally agitated.

Be flexible. One of the most amazing things about teachers' and counselors' attempts at discipline is that when they do something that doesn't work very well the first time, they persist in doing it again and again.

You yell at a child to stop punching a student in the seat next to him, yet he continues to do so. What to you do? Yell louder.

You punish a child by taking away some privilege but it has no discernible effect. So what to you do? Take away *another* privilege.

You censure a student for talking out of turn, and what does she do? She becomes even more belligerent. So what do you do? Censure her again.

The simplest solution to sorting out any conflict is to figure out what you are doing that is not working—and don't do that anymore. Do something else. *Anything* other that what you are already doing.

The hardest thing about this is that there are certain interventions, strategies, things we say and do, with which we are most comfortable. We do not like to give them up, even when they are not working. If you nag a child to do something and this has no impact on changing her behavior, rather than continuing to nag it is time to try something else. Although you may not know what will work, you assuredly know what will *not* work. You do not have to try that anymore and can devote your energies to experimenting until you find the right combination.

Counseling squared. A counseling relationship is a partnership, one in which its success depends very much on how well the participants are functioning together. Just as couples seek marital counseling when they are not getting along, or adversaries seek mediation when they have reached an impasse, one creative solution to an irreconcilable conflict is to recruit some assistance from an outside source—that is, to double the resources available in the session.

I discovered this strategy one time when a colleague was going on vacation and he asked me to take a few of his cases while he was gone. He warned me that with a few students in particular he had reached the end of his resources, and he welcomed anything I could do to improve the situations. Not wanting to engage in any deep-level counseling that might conflict with the work my colleague was already doing, I instead concentrated my efforts on asking the students to consider ways they could work harder and more effectively with their counselor once he returned. To my surprise, the students were most forthcoming and honest: They disclosed all the things they did not like about their sessions and shared exactly what they thought their counselor could do differently that would help them to open up more. Furthermore, they gave me permission to pass the advice along to him.

A few days after my colleague returned, he called to tell me about the breakthroughs that occurred with the students I had seen. The simple act of seeing a mediator, a neutral party, made a tremendous difference in breaking through the impasse that he had been experiencing with these students. This gave me the idea to expand the strategy further.

I had been having difficulty with a student of my own, a surly adolescent who refused to talk in our sessions; he would just pick at his face, scowl menacingly at me, and occasionally grunt. After the third session, there was overt hostility between us. Each of us felt angry and resentful toward the other, determined to win this struggle. Even worse, we were stuck with one another.

As a lark, one day I invited one of my officemates to join us in a session. Mostly my intention was to show him how offensive this young man was, but during a moment of inspiration I decided instead to introduce him by saying to my colleague, "Look, we need some help. We seem to be stuck. Neither one of us particularly wants to work with the other but we do not have a lot of choice here. We have more sessions scheduled together and neither of us is particularly looking forward to them. I wonder if there is something that you can do to help us work things out? We need some marital counseling."

The boy smirked at that, but I could see he agreed. Actually, he was shocked at the way I presented things—I didn't blame him for our problems but rather framed the conflict as a circumstance that seemed to be beyond *our* control. After this introduction, it didn't matter so much what my colleague did with us. Verbalizing the notion that we owned our problems together and definitely needed some help to sort things out created a necessary shift in our work together. When the "visiting counselor" asked us to identify the main problems, what each of us was doing to contribute to these conflicts, and what we could each do differently, we were well on our way to sorting things out. Ever since that time, I have seen a lot of benefits to inviting a mediator into sessions when an obvious impasse has been reached. Sometimes that co-counselor can even be a friend of the student, someone who is willing to act on his or her behalf.

Let go. There are times when you can drive yourself crazy trying to fix someone who doesn't want to be fixed. In spite of how skilled and knowledgeable you are, how dedicated and motivated, there are limits to what you can do. If a student is bound and determined to act disruptively, for whatever reason, sometimes the best you can do is minimize the damage to yourself and others for whom you are responsible. Sometimes it is better to do less, rather than more.

It is senseless to argue with someone who likes to fight. There is no way you can win a battle of wills when the other person has nothing to lose. There are times when the best thing you can do is to simply let go of your investment in the outcome, to shrug your shoulders and tell the student (and yourself) that now just doesn't seem to be the best time to offer help. Perhaps sometime in the future things might proceed more successfully.

Strategic Interventions

In addition to the general rules of engagement, there are a number of other strategies that often prove useful when working with cases you find challenging. Combining the work of problem-solving therapists such as Steve de Shazer (1991), William O'Hanlon (Cade & O'Hanlon, 1994), and Michelle Weiner-Davis; strategic therapists such as Jay Haley and Chloe Madanes; and narrative therapists such as David Epston and Michael White, a number of interventions are often useful in breaking down barriers.

Time is the school counselor's greatest enemy; there is precious little of it available to complete all the necessary daily administrative tasks, much less service several hundred students on your caseload. The children showing overt signs of problems alone would keep a medium-sized community agency staff busy indefinitely. It is obvious, therefore, that school counselors must devise ways to intervene efficiently with students who are having difficulty. The luxury of seeing clients in private practice for consecutive months, or even for a half dozen sessions, may have sounded good back in graduate school, but it just isn't feasible in the life of a typical school counselor.

Although counselors in school settings have been doing brief counseling, even single-session treatment, for decades, it has not been until recent times that attempts have been made to initiate this process systematically.

Keep in mind that brief counseling methods are not at odds with the relationship-oriented work we already do. In fact, Bruce (1995) makes the point that brief school counseling interventions are far more likely to be successful when there is a solid alliance with the child, the counselor listens carefully and nonjudgmentally in order to understand the child's worldview, there is collaborative support within a respectful climate, and the student's strengths rather than weaknesses are emphasized.

For brief, strategic techniques to work, they must be applied within a particular context that subscribes to several assumptions:

1. The problem is the problem. In other words, treat the presenting complaint rather than try to figure out what the "real" underlying issue may be.
2. Make sure the identified problem is one that both the student and complainant agree is disturbing. It does little good

to work on an issue unless both the child and the teacher/ parent/administrator agree that such efforts are appropriate.

3. Difficult behavior results from circular causality. There are interactive effects implicit in any interactive struggle; one person sparks reactions in the other, which in turn elicits other responses.

4. Disturbing symptoms represent the child's attempt to solve the problem. All behavior is functional on some level. Each of us is doing the best we can with what we know how to do. Find out who the child is helping or protecting as a result of acting out.

5. Difficult students are stuck. They do not see other alternatives that work as well as what they are already doing.

6. Adopt a cautious and respectful attitude. Maintain a "one-down" position in which you present yourself in the role of consultant rather than authority figure.

7. Focus on the future. Rather than dwell on what has already taken place, or even what is going on in the present, concentrate efforts on what *can* be done in the future.

8. Move beyond blame. First, it is impossible to determine who is solely at fault. Secondly, assigning guilt does not do anything useful to resolve the difficulty.

9. Find out as much as you can about the context of the problem. When does it occur? Where does it occur? With whom does it occur? When does it *not* occur?

10. Look for exceptions. Normal counseling asks people to talk about their problems. Instead, try exploring those instances when the child is successful and doesn't engage in the disruptive behavior.

11. The child has the resources to solve the problem. Assume that given sufficient support, encouragement, and guidance the child can resolve things to everyone's satisfaction.

12. Small steps lead to big changes. Start with relatively small steps in the right direction.

13. Stay *very* flexible. Observe the current pattern before attempting any intervention. Note carefully the effects of what you are doing. Repeat what works; do not repeat what doesn't.

14. If the child isn't motivated to resolve things, then work with someone else (parents, teacher, friend).

Most of these assumptions underlie the techniques for working with challenging students described below.

The miracle question. This is a staple of many problem-solving therapists in which the student is asked to imagine a time in the future when, by some miracle, the presenting problem has been resolved. "Think about what would be different. What would your teacher/parents/friends notice? How would you feel?" And then: "How was the problem solved? What did you do?"

In the ensuing dialogue, this technique is demonstrated further:

Counselor:	Hey guy! What's been up with you?
Flynn:	Nothin'. Same ole.
Counselor:	I understand you've been having some problems lately.
Flynn:	Nah! Just a misunderstanding.
Counselor:	A misunderstanding? Seven detentions in a semester?
Flynn:	What's the use? Anything I do won't change anything.
Counselor:	I wonder if that's true. What if I could wave a magic wand and make everything better? What would things be like?
Flynn:	For one thing, everyone would be off my back. [Laughs]
Counselor:	That *would* be a miracle, huh? What else?
Flynn:	Well, I . . . You know . . . I guess I wouldn't get in trouble so much.
Counselor:	That might be a nice change of pace. What else?
Flynn:	I don't know. My parents would leave me alone. I'd be getting good grades and stuff.

Counselor: Okay. That sounds like a pretty nice future. Now, how did you make that happen?

It is at this point there is often some resistance, both because what we are asking the child to do is difficult and because whatever answer is provided is actually the "magical" solution. The consequence of articulating this out loud is that the student is actually describing exactly what he needs to do to get back on track. When the boy in the previous dialogue looked into the future, telling what he did to fix things, he described himself as someone who was responsible, in control, and perfectly capable of making good things happen. Through the counselor's guidance, the emphasis was not on what the student's teachers, friends, and parents would do differently but rather on what the student would do more effectively.

When things are going right. The problem with difficult students is that they are locked into a pattern in which everyone, including the students themselves, are always focused on what they are doing wrong. The frequency and intensity of the disruptive behavior are often exaggerated, as if the problem behavior was *always* occurring. Yet even the most belligerent student is sometimes considerate, the most withdrawn student occasionally initiates things, the most thoughtless student is known to be responsible when they perceive something is important.

Remember to ask about the times when the student is in control and doing quite well:

Counselor: So far, we've pretty much been talking only about the trouble you get into. I'd be interested to hear about the times when you are on top of things.

Karyn: If you talk to my mother or my teachers, they'll tell you I'm always in trouble for one thing or another.

Counselor: I know it sure feels that way. Perhaps they do notice you mostly when you are acting up. What I wonder, though, is what you are like when you are cooperative. Like right now, for instance. I find you very easy to talk to. What are some other times when you are doing well?

The emphasis, of course, is on balancing the negative aspects with positive aspects of the student's behavior. By emphasizing what she is capable of doing, the counselor is actually encouraging her to be more responsible.

Shake things up. If little changes lead to bigger ones, then the strategy should be to find some way to make even slight alterations in the way the student behaves. This can involve changes in the

- Rate of behavior: getting the child to repeat behavior less often or, if that isn't possible, then more often initially
- Duration of behavior: decreasing or increasing the length of time in which a child does something
- Intensity of behavior: encouraging the child to do something softer or harder
- Sequence of behavior: mixing up the order in which behaviors occur
- Location of behavior: changing the place or time of day in which the behavior occurs

By making any of these small changes, the child is demonstrating his or her capability to alter the way things are done. If we accept the systemic view that the problematic child is part of a larger interactive pattern, then even small changes in the student's behavior can spark more dramatic ones in others' behavior.

Reframing. This is another standard procedure of strategic therapists that we never can do enough of—redefining the presenting problem in a way that makes it easier to solve. For example, a very capable eighth-grade student repeatedly waits until the night before assignments are due before he begins them. As a result, the quality of his work suffers, but only to the point where it is disturbing to his parents—who schedule a conference with you.

During the session, attended not only by both parents but by the young man as well, you listen to repeated criticisms about how lazy the child is: He always waits until the last minute. He should be doing so much better in school but he just doesn't apply himself. He hardly tries.

The counselor wants to break this pattern because it is clear that repeated nagging by the parents is not having the desired effect on their child; if anything, he is becoming more entrenched in his pattern of waiting until the last minute, just to prove he cannot be controlled. The counselor offers an alternative explanation, one that describes the same situation in a different light: "It isn't that you are lazy at all. In fact, I've heard about a number of situations—like playing Little League baseball or skiing—in which you work in an extremely dedicated and consistent way to improve your skills. No, I don't think you're lazy at all. Rather, I think you just work well under pressure."

The boy breaks out into a spontaneous smile, not because he feels let off the hook but because *this* is an explanation that makes sense to him. His parents are about to disagree but then look thoughtful for a moment, considering this alternative diagnosis of the problem. Although they are not quite ready to accept it yet, they are now thinking about their son's behavior in a different way.

Challenge thinking. In the spirit of cognitively based therapies, it is critical to help many children to think differently about their predicaments. The unmotivated student, for example, is often engaging in negative self-talk such as the following:

"I suck as a student."

"It'll never be any different."

"My teachers don't like me."

"I don't care about this stuff anyway."

These self-defeating beliefs must be challenged along the lines of finding the evidence to support them. Ideally, in group settings, Campbell (1991) suggests encouraging unmotivated students to confront one another. First of all, students must learn to differentiate those times when they are passionately driven to do something from those times at school when they are not. Next, they are encouraged to confront their negative messages with alternatives:

"I could be better as a student if I really tried."

"*Some* teachers don't like the way I *act*."

"I'm afraid to care about school in case I can't succeed the way I'd prefer."

In addition to this cognitive restructuring, Lewis (1992) stresses the role of helping children discriminate between those times when they do well and those times when they do not feel motivated:

"Talk about that time in art class when your painting was displayed in front of the class. How did you manage that?"

"What happened during social studies when you stopped trying? Without blaming the teacher, what happened inside of *you*?"

"How do you account for the fact that other children do well in those situations? What's the difference?"

"How do you explain that your times are so fast in the 50-yard dash but your performance in math is so poor?"

In each case, we are helping the student to search for the internal self-perceptions that sustain negative beliefs about their capabilities. Lewis suggests that instead of waiting until children become unmotivated and blame others for their own lack of interest, counselors should be helping to prevent these problems through classroom guidance activities. Such units could include structured explorations into what generates interest in school activities. Rather than blame teachers for being boring (the most typical excuse), children are helped to develop ways they can make their own learning more dynamic. We can all think of times when other people were bored or disengaged but we weren't because of things we were doing differently. That lesson in self-responsibility can go a long way in taking the focus off others and helping students to reclaim their own responsibility.

5

What About Challenging Colleagues?

"Look. It's not so much that I don't like the way you're handling things *(read: I don't like the way you are handling things)* as I disagree with the policy that has been established. I have been your greatest advocate *(to your face; behind your back, I undermine you every chance I get)*. I really want you to be successful *(only to the extent that it makes me look good)*. You have to trust me *(don't trust me)* if you expect me to help *(help? I will make sure you fail with every resource at my disposal)*. It just pains me so to see you struggling *(pains me that I cannot see more)* and I want to run interference for you *("interfere" is just about right)*. So now, tell me what is going on with you."

Under the cloak of sincerity and apparent good intentions lurks a deceptive, manipulative individual whom you can neither trust nor open up to without covering yourself against ambush. This may be an administrator to whom you report, the parent of one of your students, a teacher or secretary in your school, or even another counselor in your department. In any case, you are forced to interact with this person on a regular basis.

The Least of Your Problems

Sometimes, uncooperative students are the least of our problems. It is, after all, children's primary job in life to test limits, entertain themselves as best they can, protect themselves from perceived assaults, and challenge adults who they believe are acting unjustly. Conflict in such circumstances is inevitable.

We were duly warned in graduate school that most of our clients might not cooperate with our best intentions. We were told about problems associated with substance abusers, victims of abuse, intractable diseases, chronic behavioral and emotional disorders, and the like. We were even led to expect that the most motivated clients would sometimes give us a hard time when they felt threatened. In fact, we learned over time that a lack of resistance may very well signal a more difficult sort of case to manage. So, as much as we might complain about how students often give us a hard time, this circumstance hardly takes us by surprise.

What does come as a shock is the extent to which some of our most challenging struggles at work have little to do with the students we see—it is our colleagues who often make life difficult.

Teachers Who Don't Understand

Teachers often do not seem to understand the roles we play and the ways we can help them. Rather than be grateful for our assistance, they may resent our intrusions. In addition, we often see them at their worst—when they are in over their heads. We hear complaints about them from students who have been sent to us, and sometimes we cannot help but feel sympathetic after learning about some of the inappropriate and unreasonable practices of teachers who probably should not be allowed in a classroom.

In one situation, you help a student dramatically improve behavior that had been considered by others to be intractable. Although the student's fourth-grade teacher should have been delighted by your assistance because the student is no longer disruptive in class, instead she feels that you demonstrated that she cannot handle her own problems. To make matters worse, rather than coming to you directly so that you might deal with this difference of opinion, she decides instead to bad-mouth you behind your back, complain about you to the principal, and even undermine the progress you made with the student who had been difficult.

You confront the teacher in a manner that is sensitive and diplomatic—even apologize for anything you did that she found offensive. Instead of putting this conflict to rest, she acts as if she doesn't know what you mean. What she is really saying to you is that she has no intention of resolving this matter—that on some level, she enjoys this struggle and intends to escalate it every chance she gets.

Administrators Who Handcuff Us

Administrators are often our greatest scourge. They assign us tasks that have nothing to do with counseling children. They use us as lackeys to take care of the chores that nobody else is willing to do. They handcuff us with rules and regulations that make it nearly impossible for us to do our jobs. Finally, they do not seem to appreciate what counseling can actually do to help children—if they did understand, surely they would do what they could to free up our time so that we could do what we were actually trained to do.

As but one example, your principal is very passive and avoids conflict at all costs, with anyone. He will not back you up during those times when you need support. He will not defend your efforts to initiate new programs in your school. He just doesn't like to make waves. When you go to him for assistance about some matter, he couldn't be more cooperative; the problem, however, is that he will not actually do anything to follow through on his promises.

As hard as you work to help the children in your school, you feel as though you are constantly hanging on a limb, one that at any moment will snap and send you crashing to the ground. You try to get the support and supervision you need elsewhere in the district, but within the school itself you feel very alone.

Parents Who Fight Us

Parents are another breed altogether. Technically, they are also our colleagues as well as the caretakers of our students. Theoretically, we should be coordinating our efforts, collaborating in constructive ways, and sharing information that makes each of our jobs flow more smoothly. They should be doing all they can to make sure their children are respectful, well fed and cared for, and eager and motivated to do their work. Certainly, this *is* the case with many families. However, every semester there are a handful of parents with whom we must deal who amaze us with their vindictiveness, abusiveness, and lack of responsibility. They blame us for being incompetent or misunderstanding their poor, unappreciated child. They scream at us for not complying with their advice. They bad-mouth us to our supervisors, and even to their own children, undercutting our authority and ability to make a difference. When all else fails, they may even threaten us with bodily harm.

In any of these situations just described, but especially with difficult parents, there are several strategies that often prove useful.

One-down position. Adopting this posture means that you do not challenge parents directly but rather solicit their help in a respectful, even pleading way. This is sometimes difficult to do because it may mean that you will have to lie a little in order to win their cooperation:

Counselor: Mr. Buzzwell, you seem to know so much more about this situation than I ever could learn. And you obviously have a number of great ideas about what I could do to better help your daughter. I wonder if you might be willing to come in for a few minutes and set me straight about what is going on. I seem to have missed some very important things to which you have alluded. I'm really interested in hearing more.

This, of course, is a very effective way to reduce conflicts with difficult parents by not challenging their competence or authority. By adopting a one-down position, we are deferring to their expertise, an invitation that is most difficult to resist.

How can I help you? Similar to the previous strategy, this attitude presumes that the difficulty we are experiencing with a particular parent exists in part because of conflict over power and control. The parent is feeling threatened by us, perhaps even ashamed about things we might know about the family or their competence as caretakers of their children.

Counselor: What I am trying to say, Mrs. Whitaker, and I'm not saying it very well, is that my job is to help you do your job better. I have it easy—I only deal with your child for a few hours per week, but you have to live with him. What I'm wondering is what I can do to help you?

There is an attitude implicit in this strategy that reminds us not to fight with parents who challenge our authority or competence. Things can quickly escalate into a yelling match, and in all such circumstances, it is the child who loses the most. We must do all we can do to charm parents into working cooperatively with us.

Introducing ideas. There are a number of things that some parents don't understand about their children. Sometimes, we can circumvent difficulties by explaining concepts that may be new to some people:

- Testing authority is normal and helpful for children.
- Children do what they have learned works best.
- Your child is doing the best she can.
- This is not your fault.

During our efforts at parent education, it is this last idea which is often most helpful of all. If parents aren't blaming us, their kids, or their kids' teachers, then they are likely blaming themselves. Our best strategy is to stop all attempts at finding fault and instead work together to find solutions.

Counselors Who Undermine Us

In addition to teachers, administrators, and parents, we get grief from our fellow counselors. Rather than protecting and supporting one another and helping each other to cope with the innumerable struggles we face every day, we sometimes are faced with colleagues who make our jobs even more difficult.

There are arguments over ideology. What is the best way to counsel children? Such a debate might even be constructive, if it was really designed to *teach* rather than *be won.* What often happens, unfortunately, is that one or more counselors believe that they are right and that everyone who doesn't subscribe to the same beliefs is incompetent or dangerous. Under such circumstances, discussions about policies and procedures are really about struggles for power. Who will control what we do and how we do it?

There are a number of very important and legitimate disagreements among counselors about such things as where time and resources should be allotted, which specialized programs should be implemented, who should take on which assigned roles, and even what the primary mission of the counseling services is. Prevention? Crisis management? Psychoeducation? Therapeutic intervention? Growth and development? Should we be acting primarily as case managers or therapists or consultants or teachers or information-management specialists, or perhaps some combination of these roles? These are certainly constructive debates—if they are conducted respectfully. And that is a big *if.*

There is competition for opportunities and resources. Counselors are often placed in a competitive situation in which there are relatively few opportunities for obtaining advancement, new resources, and the plum jobs. In some schools or districts, counselors feel compelled to make themselves look good at the expense of others.

There are personality clashes. Some people just don't get along very well with others. Actually, I am being polite. What I am really thinking about are those folks in our field who are scary. They became teachers in the first place because they like to be in control over other people's lives. Over time, they began to take themselves *very* seriously, as if they were not only important, but far brighter and more capable than anyone else. They saw counseling as a way to become trained in the skills of being manipulative and even more powerful. In a sense they were right: Counselor education does prepare us with the knowledge and skills to more effectively get others to do things they might not want to do.

These wayward colleagues, once they became counselors, developed even more rigid, narcissistic, and manipulative patterns. Perhaps you've met or worked with someone like this before. They like to play mind games. They actually enjoy conflicts—these are the times they feel most alive. They are exquisitely sensitive to each person's weaknesses and vulnerabilities and they feel no compunction about exploiting them every chance they get. Although you may have an agenda to work cooperatively with colleagues, these individuals thrive on petty squabbles, if not outright war. They like the feeling of power that comes with making other people feel as miserable as they do most of the time.

What About You?

Yes, I'm talking to *you!* It is easy to blame our colleagues for making our lives difficult, for sabotaging us, for making our jobs and lives far more difficult than they need to be. It is easy to point the finger at someone else—a neglectful principal, an ungrateful teacher, an abusive parent, or an incompetent colleague. If what I said earlier with respect to challenging children is true—that they sometimes don't come to us as difficult, we make them that way—then the same thing is possible with many of our so-called difficult colleagues.

The question to ask yourself, one that you clearly will not like, is What is *your* role in being obstructive with others? If you accept the premise that conflicts almost always result from the contributions of both parties, then you must look at what you are doing to create or exacerbate such arguments. In other words, if someone was to research systematically how you are perceived by those with whom you most often find yourself in disagreement, what would these individuals say about you?

It is highly likely there are a number of things that you say and do that consistently get you in trouble. These are patterns that have been present from your own childhood and are probably quite familiar to you and the other people who have been on the receiving end of them. In fact, it might be profitable for you to consider these recurring conflicts that you have lived through again and again in slightly different forms.

What I am suggesting to you, which is not unlike what you offer to so many of your own clients, is that we are primarily the authors of our own life stories. Certainly we must contend with other people who may be unscrupulous, unreasonable, or abusive, but these folks do not necessarily act this way with everyone—only those who either invite this behavior or ignite it through their actions.

As one example of this phenomenon, let me recount the story of a colleague who was giving me an awful time. He was undermining me every chance he got—bad-mouthing me to students, contradicting me behind my back, creating problems that I would have to solve, placing students in situations in which they would have to choose whether to be loyal to him or me. In short, he did everything he could think of to make my life difficult. Furthermore, he was an easy target to blame as he was unpleasant to others as well. This made my role as a victim even easier—I spent months feeling sorry for myself, recruiting support for my positions, cataloguing all the crazy things he was doing that I found inappropriate and unprofessional.

It got my attention, however, when I started realizing that there were indeed people around with whom he had solid, healthy relationships. So, I asked myself, what did I do to deserve his wrath? What was I doing to invite him to treat me so poorly? How was I aggravating him in ways that were coming back to haunt me?

In all honesty, I must admit that I did not like doing this one bit. In some ways, I enjoyed being a victim of his abuse—I must have, or

I wouldn't have tolerated things for so long! I also liked commiserating with allies, friends, and families about the latest indignity that I suffered. In some ways, I am reluctant to admit, I also liked doing little things that I knew would irritate the heck out of him. On some perverse level, all of this was immensely entertaining.

Once I began looking at what my role was in this conflict, I was surprised at how my sense of powerlessness vanished. I no longer felt that he was doing something *to* me, as much as we were doing some sort of weird dance together. Although this realization didn't offer me any clues as to how I could get him to treat me any differently, it did suggest some new ways that I could conceptualize the conflict. No longer would I blame him for acting like a jerk, because he clearly acted in that manner only with those people who interacted with him in certain ways.

Of course, this pattern was familiar to me in my life. I could recall others with whom I had been locked into similar dynamics. I hadn't been all that successful previously in working through these struggles, but this time I was determined to do things differently. I cannot say, in all honesty, that I ever did get this guy to stop his behavior completely. I tried setting limits. I experimented with various ways of responding to him. Nothing worked very well except what I did inside my own head: I stopped blaming him for doing the best he could. I eventually left this job, partially to get away from him. You probably aren't surprised to learn that he showed up again in a slightly altered form in every other job I have had since then. What I hope is different now, however, is that I am much more interested in looking at what I do to invite conflicts rather than at what other people do that I find so disagreeable.

There are limits, however, to the extent to which you can take responsibility for difficult relationships, especially when you are dealing with people who become abusive.

Those Who Abuse You

"I DON'T CARE WHAT YOU THOUGHT I MEANT: I AM TELLING YOU RIGHT NOW WHAT I WANT—NO, WHAT I *DEMAND* THAT *YOU DO.* I WILL *NOT* QUIET DOWN AND I AM *NOT* OUT OF CONTROL. I am just trying to get through to you.

You obviously have a hard time understanding even the most basic instructions and it burns my ass that you do not listen. I am trying to be reasonable with you, but that is quite difficult with someone who is so deficient in as many areas as you are. That is why, you sorry sack of shit, I have to resort to being a little loud in order to get your attention."

"HOW DARE YOUR QUESTION MY MOTIVES! IF YOU WANT SOME TROUBLE, I'LL GIVE YOU MORE THAN YOU CAN HANDLE. Do we understand one another?"

People who are abusive almost cannot help themselves. Their violence, aggressiveness, unbridled anger, and lashing out at others results from poor impulse control. They believe very strongly that other people are at fault for almost everything. Blame is a way of life for these individuals:

"If only you would have listened to me the first time, I would not have had to resort to such extreme measures."

"If you would just do your job the way I asked you to do it, then I would not have to yell."

"You made me so mad I had no choice but to teach you a lesson."

"You should know better than to do that; you know what it does to me. Gee, I'm sorry I got a little carried away. Are you alright?"

There are times when other people in your life, whether they are staff members in your school, students, parents of your students, or your own family and friends, consistently create disturbances that draw you in. In spite of your best efforts to negotiate some sort of truce, the interactions with these people remain uncomfortable, even distasteful.

You do not feel respected, nor do you feel that the other person is all that interested in getting along.

Even when you cannot control other people or dictate that they abide by your rules, or when you find yourself unable to live up to their demands, you can assuredly function in such a way that you do not place yourself in such a vulnerable position. In order to work such conflicts through, there are several ways that you may wish to reorient your perspective on these relationships:

1. Think in terms of interactive effects and mutual responsibility rather than who did what to whom and who is the biggest villain.
2. Stop thinking in terms of winning and losing, but rather adopt an attitude that assumes both of you can get part of what you want.
3. Refuse to engage in or tolerate verbal abuse, physical violence, or destructive aggression.
4. Establish and enforce firm but reasonable limits during communication and emphasize respectful attention, responsive listening, and compromise.
5. Use a number of tactics and strategies that combine positions of power (assertiveness, threat, coercion, confrontation) and concession (compromise, compliance, empathy).
6. Remain flexible in your thinking and in your actions so that you are in a position to settle a conflict in a maximum number of different ways.
7. Remain committed to the notion that you can get much of what you want without antagonizing your adversary in such a way that continued conflict is likely.

In Summary

I wish to close our discussion of working with challenging people by reviewing and reframing a few principles we have discussed:

1. Challenging people make your life interesting. They are inventive, creative, passionate, and feel very strongly about their beliefs, which may differ from your own.
2. They help us to look at our own need for control. Many of us became counselors in the first place because we like being in

control. We do not take kindly to others—especially people smaller than us—trying to challenge our authority.

3. Students who we find difficult are not necessarily being resistant; they are simply cooperating in ways that are different from what we expect.

References and Suggested Readings

Amatea, E. S. (1989). *Brief strategic interventions for school behavior problems.* San Francisco: Jossey-Bass.

Bonnington, S. B. (1993). Solution-focused brief therapy: Helpful interventions for school counselors. *The School Counselor, 41,* 126-128.

Bruce, M. A. (1995). Brief counseling: An effective model for change. *The School Counselor, 42,* 353-363.

Cade, B., & O'Hanlon, W. H. (1994). *A brief guide to brief therapy.* New York: Norton.

Campbell, C. A. (1991). Group guidance for academically under-motivated children. *Elementary School Guidance and Counseling, 25,* 302-307.

Carns, A. W., & Carns, M. R. (1994). Making behavioral contracts successful. *The School Counselor, 42,* 155-160.

de Shazer, S. (1991). *Putting differences to work.* New York: Norton.

Downing, J., & Downing, S. (1991). Consultation with resistant parents. *Elementary School Guidance and Counseling, 25,* 296-301.

Downing, J., & Harrison, T. C. (1990). Dropout prevention: A practical approach. *The School Counselor, 38,* 67-74.

Kottler, J. A. (1992). *Compassionate therapy: Working with difficult clients*. San Francisco: Jossey-Bass.

Kottler, J. A. (1994). *Beyond blame: A new way of resolving conflicts in relationships*. San Francisco: Jossey-Bass.

Kottler, J. A., Sexton, T., & Whiston, S. (1994). *The heart of healing: Relationships in therapy*. San Francisco: Jossey-Bass.

Lewis, A. (1992). Student motivation and learning: The role of the school counselor. *The School Counselor, 39*, 333-337.

Littrell, J. M., Malia, J. A., & Vanderwood, M. (1995). Single-session brief counseling in a high school. *Journal of Counseling and Development, 73*, 451-458.

Molnar, A., & Lindquist, B. (1990). *Changing problem behavior in the schools*. San Francisco: Jossey-Bass.

Murphy, J. J. (1994). Working with what works: A solution-focused approach to school behavior problems. *The School Counselor, 42*, 59-65.

Peeks, B. (1992). Protection and social context: Understanding a child's problem behavior. *Elementary School Guidance and Counseling, 26*, 295-304.

Ritchie, M. (1994). Counseling difficult children. *Canadian Journal of Counseling, 28*, 58-68.

Roth, H. J. (1991). School counseling groups for violent and assaultive youth: The Willie M.'s. *Journal of Offender Rehabilitation, 16*, 113-131.

Seligman, L., & Gaaserud, L. (1994). Difficult clients: Who are they and how do we help them? *Canadian Journal of Counseling, 28*, 25-42.

Webb, W. (1992). Empowering at-risk children. *Elementary School Guidance and Counseling, 27*, 96-103.

Willison, B. G., & Masson, R. L. (1990). Therapeutic reparenting for the developmentally deprived student. *The School Counselor, 38*, 143-152.

Index

CORWIN
PRESS

The Corwin Press logo—a raven striding across an open book—represents the happy union of courage and learning. We are a professional-level publisher of books and journals for K-12 educators, and we are committed to creating and providing resources that embody these qualities. Corwin's motto is "Success for All Learners."